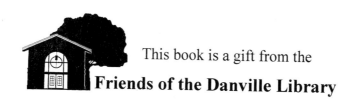

This book is a gift from the

Friends of the Danville Library

THE GREEN BAY PACKERS

Sloan MacRae

PowerKiDS press

New York

Published in 2011 by The Rosen Publishing Group, Inc.
29 East 21st Street, New York, NY 10010

First Edition

Editor: Amelie von Zumbusch
Book Design: Greg Tucker
Layout Design: Julio Gil

Photo Credits: Cover (Don Hutson), p. 13 Hulton Archive/Getty Images; cover (Aaron Rodgers), p. 21 Tom Dahlin/Getty Images; cover (Jim Taylor), p. 5 James Flores/Getty Images; cover (background), p. 9 Jonathan Daniel/Getty Images; p. 7 Matt Sullivan/Getty Images; p. 11 Scott Boehm/Getty Images; pp. 15, 22 (top) Vernon Biever/Getty Images; p. 17 Walter Iooss Jr./Sports Illustrated/Getty Images; pp. 19, 22 (bottom) Ron Vesely/Getty Images.

Library of Congress Cataloging-in-Publication Data

MacRae, Sloan.
  The Green Bay Packers / by Sloan MacRae. — 1st ed.
     p. cm. — (America's greatest teams)
  Includes index.
  ISBN 978-1-4488-2579-0 (library binding) — ISBN 978-1-4488-2747-3 (pbk.) — ISBN 978-1-4488-2748-0 (6-pack)
  1. Green Bay Packers (Football team)—History—Juvenile literature. I. Title.
  GV956.G7M34 2011
  796.332'640977561—dc22

                                       2010034811

Manufactured in the United States of America

CPSIA Compliance Information: Batch #WW11PK: For Further Information contact Rosen Publishing, New York, New York at 1-800-237-9932

CONTENTS

THE LITTLE CITY THAT COULD

Most **professional** football teams play in big cities, such as New York or Chicago. Big cities bring teams more fans and more money. Green Bay, Wisconsin, is not a big city. However, it is home to one of the greatest teams in all of American sports.

The Green Bay Packers have played in the same city longer than any other team in the National Football **League**, or the NFL, has. The Packers have won more **titles** than any other NFL team. Green Bay might be small, but it earned the nickname Titletown thanks to its great football team. Some of the greatest **coaches** and players of all time have been Packers.

Fullback Jim Taylor (right) is one of many great Packers players. Here, he takes part in the very first Super Bowl.

OWNED BY THE PEOPLE

It is not easy to run a professional sports team. Many teams struggle to stay in business. Some are forced to move to bigger cities. The Packers have struggled to stay in business at times. Today, though, they are one of the strongest teams in America. One reason for the Packers' success is that the community owns the team. The people of Green Bay are proud of their football team. They will do anything to keep the team where it is.

The Green Bay colors are green, white, and a shade of yellow called gold. The Packers **logo** is a big letter *G* that stands for "Green Bay."

You can see the Packers' team colors on the uniforms they most often wear. If you look at the helmets they generally wear, you can see their logo.

CHEESEHEADS

The Packers play in a **stadium** called Lambeau Field. Curly Lambeau helped form the Green Bay Packers. He later served as the team's coach. The stadium is named after him.

Wisconsin gets very cold in the fall and winter. The cold does not keep Packers fans from crowding Lambeau Field. Some fans wear funny hats shaped like pieces of cheese. They do this because Wisconsin is known for its cheese. Packers fans are often called Cheeseheads.

Cheeseheads do not live only in Green Bay. They come from all across the nation. Many people believe that the Packers have the best **fan base** in the NFL.

These Packers fans are ready for a game. They have cheese hats, Packers shirts, and green and yellow beads. They even painted their faces!

9

THE INDIAN PACKING COMPANY

The Packers got their start in 1919, when two friends named Curly Lambeau and George Calhoun decided to form a football team. Unlike many people who form sports teams, Lambeau and Calhoun were not rich. Lambeau worked for the Indian Packing Company. He asked his bosses to give the team money to buy jerseys, or shirts with numbers on them. The Indian Packing Company gave Lambeau the money. They said the team had to be called the Green Bay Packers, though.

The Packers got off to a good start. In 1921, they joined the new American Professional Football Association. This group would become today's NFL.

This statue of Curly Lambeau stands outside of Lambeau Field. Lambeau not only helped found the team, he also played for and coached the Packers!

CHAMPIONS

Today the **Super Bowl** is the biggest football game of the year. The team that wins it is the NFL **champion**. The Packers were champions long before the Super Bowl was invented, though. Stars such as Red Dunn and Johnny "Blood" McNally led Green Bay to its first championship in 1929. The Packers won two more championships in 1930 and 1931. They were the first team to win the title three years in a row.

The great Don Hutson joined the team in 1935. Some football teams did not want Hutson because they thought that he was too small. He proved them wrong. He helped the Packers win more championships in 1936, 1939, and 1944.

Don Hutson held 18 NFL records when he stopped playing in 1945. He is still considered one of the best wide receivers in football history.

13

LOMBARDI

No team stays great forever, and the Packers struggled in the 1950s. They needed a new leader. They found one in 1959, when Vince Lombardi became the head coach. It took him only two seasons to lead the Packers back to the **play-offs**. Lombardi worked well with **quarterback** Bart Starr. They led the Packers to championships in 1961, 1962, and 1965.

The Packers even won the very first Super Bowl at the end of the 1966 season. They won the Super Bowl again the next year. Lombardi was such an excellent coach that today the Super Bowl **trophy** is named after him.

Here, Vince Lombardi (center) talks about plays with Bart Starr. Lombardi was named the coach of the year in both 1959 and 1961.

BACK ON TOP

Lombardi left the Packers in 1969. The team fell on hard times after that. Green Bay went through five head coaches over the next 22 years. Not even Bart Starr could turn the team around. The Packers did not return to greatness until the 1990s.

Head coach Mike Holmgren and quarterback Brett Favre joined the team in 1992. Favre soon became one of the best **offensive** players in NFL history. In 1993, Reggie White became a Packer. White was one of the greatest **defensive** players ever. White and Favre led the Packers back to the Super Bowl in 1997. They beat the New England Patriots.

Here, Reggie White (right) is playing in Super Bowl XXXI on January 26, 1997. In that game, White set a Super Bowl record by making three sacks.

GREAT QUARTERBACKS

Brett Favre did more than help the Packers win another championship. He was so famous that he became the face of the NFL. Football is a hard sport. Players get hurt during the season. Most players have to sit out of games at some point. Brett Favre set an NFL record by starting the most games in a row as quarterback. With more than 200 starts, many fans believe his record will never be broken.

Favre left the Packers in 2008. Back-up quarterback Aaron Rodgers took his place. It did not take Rodgers long to set records of his own.

Favre was named the NFL's most valuable player, or MVP, in 1995 and 1996. In 1997, he shared the title of MVP with Detroit Lions player Barry Sanders.

TITLETOWN

Green Bay might not be a big city, but it has a very big football team. The Packers have won more championships than any other team in the NFL. Fans love the Packers because they prove that the biggest cities do not always have the best teams.

Many of the best players and coaches of all time have been Packers. The names change, but the Packers continue to be great. After Favre left the team, Rodgers became the first person in NFL history to throw for 4,000 yards in his first two seasons as starting quarterback. He and the Packers are still the heroes of Titletown. The Cheeseheads will pack Lambeau Field for many years to come.

Aaron Rodgers joined the Green Bay Packers in 2005. He was the back-up quarterback for several years before becoming a big star.

21

GREEN BAY PACKERS TIMELINE

1919

Curly Lambeau and George Calhoun form a football team together.

1921

The Packers join the professional football league that would become the NFL.

1929

The Packers win their first NFL championship.

1935

Don Hutson plays his first regular-season game as a Packer.

1959

Vince Lombardi has his first season as the head coach and general manager of the Packers.

1967

The Packers beat the Kansas City Chiefs in the very first Super Bowl.

1997

The Packers beat the New England Patriots in the Super Bowl.

2008

Brett Favre plays his last game as a Green Bay Packer.

2010

Aaron Rodgers becomes the first NFL quarterback to throw for 4,000 yards in his first two seasons as a starting quarterback.

GLOSSARY

CHAMPION (CHAM-pee-un) The best, or the winner.

COACHES (KOHCH-ez) People who direct teams.

DEFENSIVE (DEE-fent-siv) Playing in a position that tries to keep the other team from scoring.

FAN BASE (FAN BAYS) The group of people who back a team.

LEAGUE (LEEG) A group of sports teams.

LOGO (LOH-goh) A picture, words, or letters that stand for a team or company.

OFFENSIVE (O-fent-siv) Playing in a position in which you try to score points.

PLAY-OFFS (PLAY-ofs) Games played after the regular season ends to see who will play in the championship game.

PROFESSIONAL (pruh-FESH-nul) Having players who are paid.

QUARTERBACK (KWAHR-ter-bak) A football player who directs the team's plays.

STADIUM (STAY-dee-um) A place where sports are played.

SUPER BOWL (SOO-per BOHL) The championship game of NFL football.

TITLES (TY-tulz) Wins that make a team the best in its sport.

TROPHY (TROH-fee) An award that is often made of metal and shaped like a cup.

INDEX

WEB SITES

Due to the changing nature of Internet links, PowerKids Press has developed an online list of Web sites related to the subject of this book. This site is updated regularly. Please use this link to access the list:
www.powerkidslinks.com/teams/fpackers/